INTRODUCTION by Sue Gifford

What are number lines?

A number line is basically any kind of line with numbers along it, spaced at equal intervals. The intervals are usually marked out with short vertical strokes called markers. As with a ruler, it is these intervals – or "steps" – which are being counted. The number line typically starts at 0 (zero), with 1 coming after the first interval.

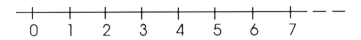

For young children this can be a source of confusion: they tend to want to count the marks, not the intervals. (The same thing can happen with rulers: some children will maintain that it is the little marks on the ruler that represent the centimetres, not the gaps between them.) It is highly understandable that children should want to count things rather than empty spaces. However, this leads to the error of counting the first mark when "counting on": for instance, a child starts at 5 and tries to count on three, but says "five, six, seven", and then declares that 7 is three more than 5. Many young children do the same thing when playing board games: if they throw a six, they count the square they are on as "one", and then move on only five.

Taking real steps along a floor number line can help children to sort out this confusion, as they are actually counting physical actions made with the w on the line. Child using dice to det they take along t.. .. .. showing, say, the numbers 0, 1 and 2, they gain experience of moving "no steps", in contrast with moving one or more steps. You can also ask children to count while you step slowly along the line, reminding them to count only after you have completed each step. Later on they can play games where they count small figures stepping along a table top line.

Number lines and number tracks

Number tracks are found on many board games, such as Snakes and Ladders, and are also available commercially. Number tracks have the numbers placed in the middle of squares or blocks, thus

1	2	3	4	5	6	7	8	9

While number tracks can be useful, they also have disadvantages. One is that the blocks on a number track are very significant and it can be tempting for a child using a number track to count these blocks rather than invisible steps. Another is that they cannot be used to represent fractions. With a number line, it is possible to use half intervals (or intervals that are worth $1/2$!) to represent halves, and similarly with other fractions.

Another feature of the number line is that it clearly represents zero as the start of the line. If zero is shown on a number track, it has to be used to mark a block. This produces the rather nonsensical image of zero marking an object – the block.

With zero in the middle of a number line, negative numbers can also be represented.

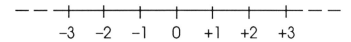

Number tracks can be useful for representing the order of numbers. They can be a lot of fun, as with board games, or numbered carpet tiles which can be moved around and jumped on. Number lines, however, are far more versatile, and can be developed to represent many sophisticated ideas about the number system.

Why use number lines?

Number lines can help children to develop an understanding of the number system, a facility for mental arithmetic and a general "feeling for number". They provide an important visual image which helps us to make sense of the number system. Many people find it useful to think of numbers stretching away into infinity in a line. It has been found that individuals develop different personal number lines, which often have bumps or zig-zags at the tens or hundreds. Sometimes the numbers go up a ladder as they get higher, an image which is also used in the "number ladders" available for working with young children.

Visualising the arrangement of tens and hundreds along a number line can help children build up an understanding of place value. This is an alternative image to that provided by base ten blocks such as Dienes' apparatus, where numbers build up in little cubes, sticks, squares and big cubes. Some people prefer to think of numbers on a line, stretching away into infinity, rather than building up into larger and larger solid blocks.

The way numbers "work" on calculators seems to fit better with a number line model of the number system, than with a "blocks" model. Children repeatedly adding ten on the calculator can easily represent this by drawing jumps on a number line. Some children seem naturally to evolve their own mental number line, in order to help them make sense of numbers they meet on a calculator, particularly large numbers and negative numbers.

Many people find it natural to use a number line image to do mental arithmetic. Try asking people to solve problems such as 54 – 48, or 85 – 27 mentally, and then ask them how they worked them out. You may find a variety of methods, but many people will have used "counting on". Some will be aware of using a mental number line, and will even describe going over some kind of bump when they come to seventy, or other tens numbers. Sometimes people imagine a vertical subtraction "sum", as if they were writing the problem down. This is not usually a very efficient method for solving problems mentally, and results from too much concentration on written calculation in childhood, and not enough work with apparatus such as number lines which can help build up other, more versatile, methods of mental calculation. A mental number line, and a facility for counting on in tens, are useful resources for children to develop in order to be able to calculate mentally. Learning to use a physical number line can help children to develop a facility for counting on mentally.

A number line provides a very flexible image of the number system. The scale and numbering of the intervals can be varied, so that a blank line can be used to represent thousands at one extreme, or decimal fractions at another. Negative numbers, as mentioned above, are soon encountered on a calculator, and these can be represented easily on a number line, so that even quite young children can investigate them.

Similarities and differences between number systems from a variety of cultures can also be explored by using number lines. Children can look at, say, a line numbered with Bengali numerals and explore similarities and differences with the internationally used numbers. Is ten a significant number in the Bengali system? What patterns are common to both?

Number lines can also be adapted to fit systems other than base ten. For instance, time lines can be related to digital clocks, 24 hour clocks, or years and centuries.

Where to buy number lines

At present the best range of number lines is available from Harcourt Brace Jovanovich (telephone: 081 300 3322). They sell all the lines originally developed by the Inner London Education Authority, including numbered and unnumbered portable lines, wall lines, and *Flexilines* which have many uses, such as being used to make floor lines for children to walk along.

Harcourt Brace Jovanovich also sell number cards, which are useful adjuncts to number line activities.

NOTE – Using number lines with children in the early years

Nursery children and others working at level 1 and below need to play freely with a variety of number lines and tracks as with any other mathematical equipment. Unnumbered lines and tracks are especially valuable as they can be used to make games and activities relating to other classroom activities. Floor lines and tracks are also useful, and attractive to children – you can provide both numbered and unnumbered ones.

Sometimes it is appropriate to talk with children about their activities with number lines and tracks, or to offer particular activities such as those offered in this booklet – but only you can decide when to intervene and when to leave children to their own play.

NUMBERS IN ORDER *USING UNNUMBERED LINES*

NATs

1,2	level 1	(*Using a floor line with 11 markers*) Here are some cards, each with a number from 0 to 10. Take steps along the line starting from the first marker, to find where the numbers should go. Do all the numbers fit on? Where will the 5 go? And the 7? What about 0? Why does 1 go where it does?
1,2	level 1	(*Using a floor line with 11 or more markers*) Play **Secret Steps**: pick a number card in secret and do that many steps along the line. See if the others can guess your number.
1,2	level 2	(*Using a table top line with 101 markers*) Can you write in the numbers to 20? or 50? or 100?
1,2	level 2	(*Using a table top line with 101 markers*) Play **Fit Them In**: Take turns picking a card from the 0-100 pack and writing in that number at the correct place. Do they all fit? Where does the 0 belong?
1,2	level 2	(*Using a line with 101 markers*) Use a calculator to help you write numbers on the line up to 20 or 30. For instance, to find out how to write the number after 10, press $\boxed{1}$ $\boxed{0}$ $\boxed{+}$ $\boxed{1}$ $\boxed{=}$ and the calculator will show eleven. If you press $\boxed{=}$ again it will show twelve; press $\boxed{=}$ again to get thirteen, and so on. *
1,2	levels 2,3	Could you make up your own number line or track winding round the classroom or going down the corridor?
1,2	levels 2-4	(*Using a line with 11 markers, well spaced*) If the first marker is 0 and the last is 10, where would you put $2\frac{1}{2}$? What about $3\frac{1}{2}$? and $5\frac{1}{4}$? Here are some counters with fractional numbers written on them. Take turns to place them in the right position on the line. Now swop two of them around and challenge a friend to find which two you moved.

* Some calculators do this if you press $\boxed{+}$ $\boxed{+}$ $\boxed{1}$ $\boxed{=}$

1,2	level 3	Here are numbers nought to ten in Bengali script. Can you put them on the line? Can you work out how to write the numbers over ten?
1,2	level 3	(*Using a line with 101 markers*) Can you make a line that starts at 100? Again, use a calculator to help you, by pressing $\boxed{1}\ \boxed{0}\ \boxed{0}\ \boxed{+}\ \boxed{1}\ \boxed{=}$ and keep pressing $\boxed{=}$.
1,2	level 3	(*Using a line with 101 markers*) Can you make a line that starts at 0 and goes up in tens to 1000? Make the calculator count in tens by pressing $\boxed{+}\ \boxed{1}\ \boxed{0}\ \boxed{=}$
1,2	levels 3,4	(*Using a line with 11 markers*) Can you put decimal numbers on the line? If the first marker is 0, and the last marker is 1, where would 0.7 go? And 0.9? What about 0.95?
1,2	levels 3,4	(*Using a line with 101 markers*) The first marker is 0 and the last is 10! Write a list of jumbled decimal numbers for a friend to fit on the line. What are the intervals worth?
1,2	levels 3,4	Use a calculator to help you make a line that has zero as the middle number. What buttons will you press? What will the numbers on the left of zero be like?
1,2	levels 3,4	Write the numbers from your negative/positive number line (see activity above) onto cards, and challenge a friend to put them in the correct places on an unnumbered line.
1,2	level 4	(*Using a line with 101 markers*) Can you make a line that goes up in hundreds to 10 000? You will need a fine-pointed pen.
1,2	levels 5,6	(*Using a line with 11 markers*) Can you put fractional numbers on the line? If the first marker is 0, and the last marker is 1, where would $^3/_8$ go? And $^2/_7$? What are the equivalent decimal numbers for these?

HOPS, STEPS AND JUMPS *USING VARIOUS NUMBERED AND UNNUMBERED LINES*

NATs

1,2	level 1	*(Using an unnumbered floor line)* Put a coloured bean bag on each marker. Start from 0, and count how many steps it is to the red bag. How many steps do you think it will be from the red bag to the green one? How many steps will it be back from the red bag to 0?
1,2	levels 1,2	*(Using a floor line numbered 0 to 10)* **Left and Right Hops 1**: Start at 0 and hop to 5 on one leg and from there to 10 on the other leg. How many left-leg hops did you do? And how many right-leg hops? Find some more ways of reaching 10 using left and right hops.
1,2	levels 1,2	*(Using a floor line numbered 0 to 10)* **Left and Right Hops 2**: How many different way can you get from 0 to 7 using different hops? Can you find a way of recording these? (*Children might use the record sheets at the back of this book.*) How many different ways are there? Now choose another number to try.
1,2	levels 1,2	*(Using a floor line numbered 0 to 10)* **Left and Right Hops 3**: Do some left-leg hops followed by some right-leg hops. What are all the different ways to get to 6 like this? How many different ways are there for 3? or 5? Can you predict how many ways there would be for 4? or 10?
1,2	levels 1,2	*(Using a line numbered 0 to 10)* How many steps does it take you to get from 10 back to 6? And 3? Guess before you do it.
1,2,5	levels 2,3	*(Using a line numbered 0 to 20)* Toss two standard dice, and draw steps for those numbers along the line, one after the other.

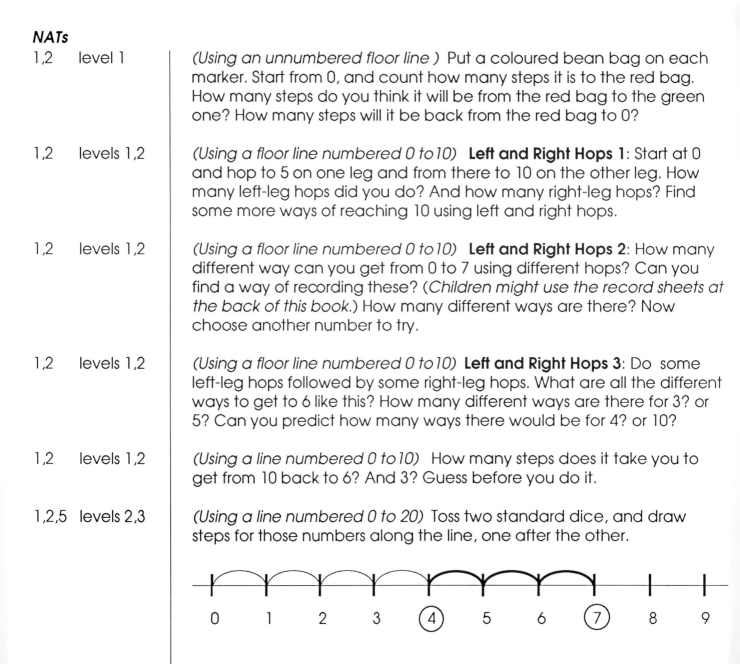

0   1   2   3   ④   5   6   ⑦   8   9

Record the final number on a graph. Do this several times. What do you notice?

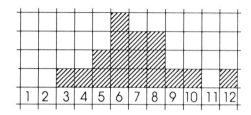

Carry on tossing and recording. Is the same thing still happening to the graph? Why is that?

What will happen if you toss the same two dice and move forwards for the larger number and back for the smaller number? Try doing this and graphing the results.

1,2   levels 2,3

(*Using a line numbered 0 to 20*) Draw three jumps of four above the line, and four jumps of three below the line. What do you notice? Can you explain why three fours and four threes should come to the same? What about other pairs of numbers? Can you see why three tens should come to the same as ten threes?

1,2,3   levels 2,3

(*Using a line numbered 0 to 50*) **Step Twice**: Pick a number from 0 to 10, start at 0, and take that many steps twice. Ring the final number.

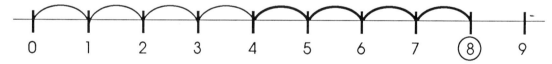

Do this several times. What do you notice about the numbers you have ringed? Can you see a pattern? Can you predict how it will continue?

1,2,3   levels 2,3

(*Using a line numbered 0 to 50*) **Step Thrice**: Pick a number and make that many steps three times. Do this several times, with different numbers, ringing the numbers you end on. What do you notice this time? Can you see a pattern to continue?

RACING GAMES *USING A RANGE OF NUMBERED AND UNNUMBERED LINES*

NATs

1,2	levels 1,2	(*Using a line numbered 0 to 100*) **Race to 100**: The aim is to be the first to reach the end of the line. Put your counters on 0, and take it in turns to toss a dice to find out how far to move. What will you do if you are on 99 and you throw a 2? Make up your own rule to decide.
1,2	levels 1,2	(*Using a line numbered 0 to 100*) Play **Race to 100** but draw your steps with felt-tipped pens.
1,2	levels 1,2	(*Using a line numbered 0 to 100*) **Race to 100 Again**: This time don't draw your steps – just put a ring around the number you land on. You could use a calculator to check that you landed on the right number.
1,2	level 2	(*Using a line numbered 0 to 100*) **Predict**: Start at 0, use two dice and move forwards for both numbers. Can you predict, before you move, and without counting the steps, where you will end up? Stay where you are, toss the dice, and move again. Go on until you reach 100, taking a cube as a prize each time you predict correctly.
1,2	level 2	(*Using a line numbered 0 to 100*) **Jump on Ten**: Each of you mark ten numbers with a blue pen. Race to 100, and when you land on one of the blue numbers, jump forwards an extra ten steps. What happens if some of the numbers you marked are in the nineties? After playing this a few times, see if you notice anything about the numbers you are jumping from and to.
1,2	level 2	(*Using a line numbered 0 to 50*) **Snake Pits**: Mark some of the numbers on the line as snake pits and toss two dice – one numbered 1 to 6 and one numbered 1, 1, 2, 2, 3, 3. You must move for the numbers you throw but for each one you can choose whether to go forwards or backwards. The aim is to reach 50 without landing in a snake pit. Decide what the penalty is if you do land in one.
1,2	levels 2,3	Make up your own game based on avoiding certain numbers.

1,2	levels 2,3	Make up a game where you go back from 100 towards 0.
1,2	levels 2,3	(*Using a line numbered 0 to 100*) **Backwards and Forwards**: Use two dice and move your counter forwards for the higher number and back towards 0 for the lower number. Can you predict where you will land before moving? Does it make any difference if you go back first, then forward? Stay where you are, toss the dice again, and move your counter again. Keep on until you reach 100.
1,2	levels 2-4	Play **Backwards and Forwards** on a line numbered –50 to +50, or one where 0 is the middle number.
1,2	levels 3,4	Make up a racing game using a number line marked in tens to 1000 and dice marked 10, 20, 30, 40, 50, 60. Or use a number line marked in hundreds to 10 000, and dice marked 100, 200, 300, 400, 500, 600.
1,2,5	levels 3-5	Make up a game using dice with higher numbers, perhaps to 9, or to 15 or 20. How does altering the numbers on the dice affect the time your game takes? A stop watch could help you to find out. Do some numbers come up less frequently than others?
1,2,3	levels 3-5	(*Using a line numbered 0 to 100*) **Double Your Number**: Race to 100, using one dice only and doubling the number it shows each time. What do you notice about the numbers you land on? What if you multiply the dice-number by three or four each time? How does this affect the time the game takes? What is a satisfactory length of time for a game?
1,2	levels 4,5	(*Using a line with 101 markers*) Make up a game where the intervals are worth 0.1, or $\frac{1}{10}$, using a spinner or cards marked 0.1, 0.2, 0.3. . .
1,2	levels 4,5	(*Using a line numbered 0 to 100*) Make up a game where the intervals are worth 0.01 or $\frac{1}{100}$.

NATs

1,2,3   levels 2,3

Build up a number pattern by arranging
- sticks in triangles (you will get 3, 6, 9. . . sticks)
- squares (you will get 4, 8, 12. . . sticks)
- handprinting (you will get 5, 10. . . fingers)
- stamping coin prints, or drawing ants or spiders

Ring the numbers on a number line. Can you describe the pattern you see?

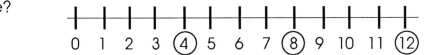

1,2,3   levels 2,3

Jump in threes along a number line and ring the numbers you land on. Write these numbers down in a list. Can you see a repeating pattern? Try jumping in fours, or fives, or some other number, and looking for repeating patterns.

1,2,3   level 3

Try jumping back from 100 in fives. What patterns can you find? Suppose you jump back in fives from 99 or some other number. Will you get a pattern this time? What will it be? Try jumping backwards in threes or sevens or tens. . .

1,2,3   level 3

When you jump in threes, you quickly get some two digit numbers. Try adding the digits in the numbers as if they were single numbers.

    12   1 + 2 = 3

    15   1 + 5 = 6

    18   1 + 8 = 9

    21   2 + 1 = 3

    24   2 + 4 = 6

Can you see a repeating pattern in the list of totals? Try with lists made by jumping in other numbers.

1,2,3	level 3	Jump in fives along the line from 0 and ring the numbers you land on. (A partner could jump in fives on a calculator to check by pressing $\boxed{+}$ $\boxed{5}$ $\boxed{=}$ $\boxed{=}$ $\boxed{=}$ *.) Say the ringed numbers aloud. Can you hear a pattern? Write the numbers down in a list. Can you see a pattern?
1,2,3	levels 3,4	Add any two numbers which are next to each other on the line, and ring the total. Do this several times with different pairs of numbers. What do you notice about the totals?
1,2,3	levels 4,5	There is a theory that whenever you add three numbers which are next to each other on the number line the number you get is in the three times table. Is this true? If so, can you explain why it happens? What happens if you add four neighbouring numbers?
1,2,3	levels 4,5	Is there any rule to be discovered about subtracting adjacent numbers?
1,2,3	levels 5,6	Find all the prime numbers to 100 and mark them on your number line. Look at the numbers adjacent to the prime numbers. What are these adjacent numbers multiples of? Why is that? What do you think will happen above 100?

* Not all calculators have this facility, called a constant function. On some calculators you press
$\boxed{+}$ $\boxed{+}$ $\boxed{5}$ $\boxed{=}$ $\boxed{=}$ $\boxed{=}$ to get the same result.

NATs

1,2,5 levels 1,2	Use the number line to show. . .

- how many people are here today, and how many are away
- how much weight each model boat held before sinking
- how much the different cakes cost in our class shop
- how many people want to play Pirates and how many want to play Pass the Parcel
- how many cars, bikes and lorries we saw passing the gate
- how many people come to school by foot, bike, car, or train

1,2,5   levels 2,3   Use the number line to work out. . .

- the total of worms, ladybirds and ants we found in our square metre
- how many children are here today if are two are away and there are thirty on the register
- how many children are having packed lunches if ten are having school dinners and two go home to dinner
- how many calculators are missing: we should have ten calculators and only six are here
- how many more people want to call the guinea pig Freda than want it called Dominic

1,2,5   levels 2,3   Estimate. . .

- how many cupfuls of water the bottle holds
- how many children there are in the school
- how many sweet papers we collected in the playground
- how much time we will all take to pack up today

Record your estimate on the number line. Now work out the correct answer, mark it on the line, and see how close your estimate was.

1,2,5   levels 2,3   Everybody estimate how many pens there are in the box and mark it on the number line. Now somebody count the pens and we will see which estimate was closest.

TIME LINES *USING UNNUMBERED LINES*

1,2,5	levels 3,4	Make a lifeline showing when you were born, and how old you are now. What important events do you want to put on it? How long have you been at school? How much of your life has been spent in your present home?
1,2,5	levels 3,4	Make a time line showing when everybody in the school was born. Who is the oldest? Who is the youngest? What age people are there most of?
1,2,5	levels 3,4	Make a time line starting from when your parents were born, or from when this school was built, or from when dinosaurs were alive, and mark on it significant events. What intervals would be best, and how many of them do you need?
1,2,5	levels 3,4	Make a time line to go with a digital clock in the classroom. Use it to work out how long you spend doing different activities, like writing or playing.
1,2,5	levels 3,4	Make a time line starting from when you wake up in the morning, until school starts, and mark on it the things you do and how long they take. What intervals would be most appropriate for this?
1,2,5	levels 3,4	Make a time line showing how you spent the last 24 hours.
1,2,5	level 4	With the aid of a TV timetable and a timeline work out how long you spend watching television during a week.
1,2,5	levels 4,5	Make a 24-hour timeline, and use a train or bus timetable to plan an outing.

NATs

1,2,3,5 levels 1-3	**Trappers**: You need ten counters and a yoghourt pot. Put the counters in the pot, then turn over the pot so some counters are trapped under it and some are outside it. Can you say how many counters are under the pot? Use the number line to help you work it out.

When you get good at it, find a partner, and challenge her to work out how many are trapped each time. Can you record what all the possibilities are?

Try with fewer or more counters to start with. What are all the possibilities this time?

1,2   level 2

Make up some sums using two numbered dice and a +/– dice. Work them out on the number line. You could try using dice that go up to 20, or dice that show ⊠ and ÷.

1,2   level 2

Differences: Two of you need 30 cubes between you. Both together toss an ordinary dice and each decide what you think is the difference between the two numbers that come up. Use the number line to check what the difference is. If you got it right, you win a cube to build a tower. Who ends up with the highest tower? Now try doing the same thing with higher numbered dice.

1,2   levels 2,3

Equal Jumps 1: Pick a number card from the pack of 0 to 100 cards. Can you get to that number from 0 in two equal jumps? Can you get to it in jumps of two? What about three equal jumps? And jumps of three?

1,2   levels 2,3

Equal Jumps 2: What numbers on the 0 to 100 line can you not get to by making equal jumps from 0?

1,2	levels 2,3	**Equal Jumps 3**: Pick a number card. Can you reach that number by making equal jumps back from 100? And from 50? Why is that?
1,2	levels 2-4	**Equal Jumps 4**: Pick a number card from the 0 to 100 pack. Can you reach that number by making equal jumps from a number other than 0? And any other number? Are there any numbers you can't reach by making equal jumps from somewhere?
1,2,3,5	level 3	Start with 20 pennies. Throw a dice numbered 1 to 6 and a +/– dice, and do what the dice tells you. For instance, if you throw plus and 6, take six. If you throw minus and 6, put back six. Go on until you have got 50 pennies, or have lost them all. Now do the same, but use a line numbered 0 to 50 instead of pennies. Now do the same on a calculator. Now do the same, but do it all in your head.
1,2	level 3	Pick four numbers under ten. Arrange these to make two two-digit numbers. Find the difference between these numbers using the number line. Now rearrange the numbers to make a different pair of numbers, and find the difference between these. Which arrangement gives you the biggest difference?
1,2	levels 4-6	Can you write a set of equations (number sentences) to show all the ways of reaching 69 in equal jumps from 0? And to show how you reach 69 in equal jumps from 1? What about reaching other numbers, and using different starting points?

Reaching 50 from 8
8 + (2 x 21)
8 + (3 x 14)
8 + (7 x 6)
8 + (6 x 7)

Reaching 69
from 0
3 x 23
23 x 3

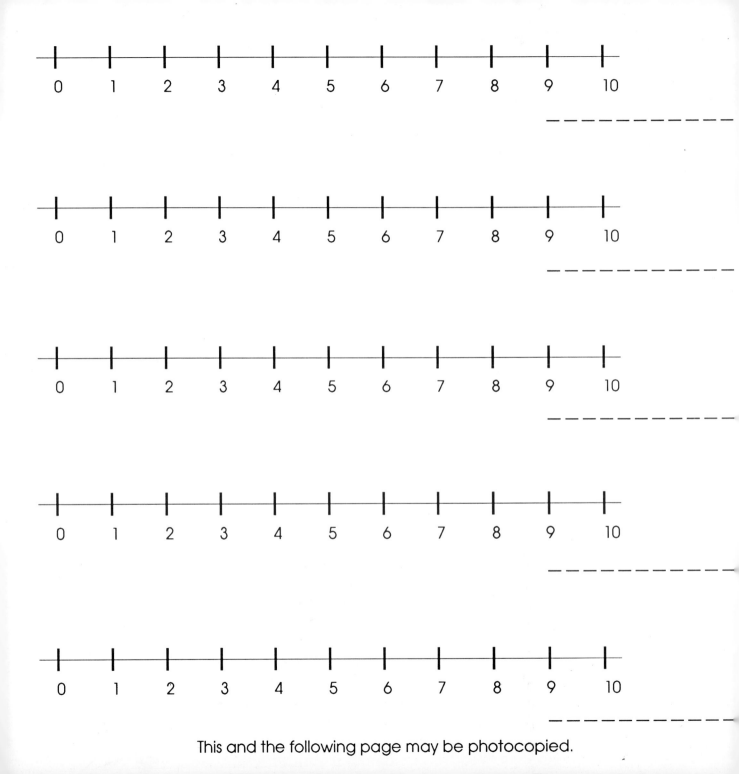

0 1 2 3 4 5 6 7 8 9 10

0 1 2 3 4 5 6 7 8 9 10

0 1 2 3 4 5 6 7 8 9 10

0 1 2 3 4 5 6 7 8 9 10

0 1 2 3 4 5 6 7 8 9 10

This and the following page may be photocopied.